GW01019176

Making it Happen

First published December 2010 by Shalom House Poetry, 31 The Cairn, Carnmoney, Newtownabbey, Co. Antrim BT36 6YF.

ISBN : 978-0-9564588-1-0

Printed by Europaprint www.europaprint.co.uk

Cover design by Michelle Taylor

This book has been published with financial support from the Small Grants Programme managed by the Arts Council for Northern Ireland

Making it Happen

An
Anthology
by
Shalom House Poetry

Acknowledgements

Shalom Writers' Group gratefully acknowledges the support of the Arts Council for Northern Ireland for its generous financial support for this publication through the Small Grants Programme.

We acknowledge also the unstinting support of Ruth Carr and Moyra Donaldson whose editorial skills and professional expertise in selecting poems for inclusion in the anthology have made it a publication of which we can be proud. The cover was designed by Michelle Taylor and her excellent work is gratefully acknowledged.

Previous Shalom House Poetry titles

Keeping the Colours New	Anthology
A View of Water	Tom Honey
Just as it Was	Pat Taylor
Pitch	Alastair Browne
The Shore Fields	Noreen Campbell
	& Denis O'Sullivan
River of Voices	Maura Rea
Love in the Time of Doubt	Jonathan Hicks
Dangerous Invitation	Elizabeth Kemp
A Christmas Mouse	Vivien Paton
A Trail of Silver Papers	Anthology
Jugglers of Light	Tom Honey

Contents

Noreen Campbell

An Áit

From the Boat Brae

a hush of quiet hangs over the island;
its people sleep.
Fields roll upwards towards velvet hills
and Lough Swilly lies lost in the early morning mist.

Around me the scent of whin and briar,
tang of bracken.
The sky lightens behind Grianan Ailech
and cattle graze in groups on the dew damp grass.

Seo é Oileán na h-Innse
an áit ar tógadh mé.

Noreen Campbell

Back Home

I'm walking the lower road,
nostalgia nipping, nudging.

At Anderson's lane, now overgrown,
a map of memories unfolds.

There, Billy's wee house stands
primly painted, blue and white.

On the right, Bohillion land
safely scatters the Cairn.

The dry stone White Wall,
burnishes with blackberry.

Now suddenly the Shore Houses,
Duffy's, Whoriskey's, Susannah's.

The houses steadfast,
the people passed on.

Noreen Campbell

Cows
for Alastair

The wind, sharp as a whip,
blew down the field
roughening hair on the cows' backs;
but they, undeterred
like ships heading for port,
grazed steadily towards the ditch
where they bunched,
backsides to the storm.

Noreen Campbell

Dream Garden

The quiet of the garden drew me in,
wrapped me in the scent of flowers,
lulled me in a sense of calm,
that came from another age.

Soon I was tiptoeing
across the stepping stones of years
to another garden,
where my mother tied back the yellow tea roses,
staked the hollyhocks to the old laburnum.
The sun shone.

I reached out to touch you, mother;
the garden disappeared
and you were gone.

Noreen Campbell

Faith

I believe in the sun though it is not shining.
I believe in the moon when the night is dark.
I believe in the wind though the trees stand still.
I believe in friends even when I am alone.
I believe in God and His ever present silence.

For Lawrence
August 16th 2007

Though a year's distance is between us
I can still see your blue eyes,
wide, trusting, unquestioning;
recall our wordless conversation,
as I watched your soul begin its journey Home.

Noreen Campbell

For Seán

I lit a candle for you today,
knelt in the quiet of the church
watched its spluttering flame;
didn't pray;
just silently said your name,
thought of your life,
and how it flickered out
twenty seven years ago.

Madge the Midwife

The funeral was on a Tuesday
the chapel packed to the door;
no relatives to fill the front seats,
just all of us, her family, in a way;
faces pale in grief, damp with tears,
hearts sore for the wee woman
who helped us into this world
and lived so long in our midst.

Odd now that it was our turn
to shoulder *her* from this world
to her place of rest.

Seventy year old Tom Doohan,
her first delivery, remarked;
poor Madge got a quick call
and her only ninety three.
She was one of the best.

Noreen Campbell

Solitude

Burning logs spill ash:
its silent crash
fills the room,
scatters sparks and shadows
through the gloom.

Denis O'Sullivan

Birthday Song

The Green Glens of Antrim trembled on the air
ninety years of remembrances spilling from
her throat.

I'm sure she was thinking of the beloved
Mountains of Mourne that shadowed her
childhood.

Or maybe of the lesser Ballynahinch Hills
that scalloped the sky behind her family
homestead.

The thrush, perhaps, and the hawthorn that
gave each other life with song and berries
in different seasons.

The crashing mountain stream brown with
bog juices and silver with Donard snow
and ice.

In the seashell I hear the wind shivering
through the pines in Tollymore and it is
her voice.

Denis O'Sullivan

Going to Mass

Granda hitched the mare to the trap,
settled himself in the driving seat,
waited at the farmyard gate,
only the clatter of hooves,
jangle of brasses
disturbing the Sabbath silence.

Granny swooshed her brood
like chickens through the door.
Boot buttons winking,
gathered black ankle length dress,
climbed the step
to take her place.

Daughters boarded next,
the young ones first, leaving
grumbling older children
pursuing Granda's "giddyup"
down the mile long lane
to the Saintfield Road.

Coming upon neighbours.
Granda said "I won't hear of ye
walking another step". By ones
and twos they were ejected,
until Granny, too, joined the ranks
trailing in the cart's wake.

Head high, she led
the walking wounded.
They bickered, they shuffled,
nursed sore feet and injured pride.
She trailed them, like a bride's train,
all the way to the altar rails.

Denis O'Sullivan

Home Visit

We loved to visit the farm at Leggygowan
where Mammy was born. Tumbling from the bus
at the end of the loaning, done with the tedium of
endless renderings of *Ten Green Bottles*, numberless
games of *I Spy*, we pushed, shoved, tasting already
Granny's sodas, hot buttered straight from the griddle.
She would be sucking a cinnamon lozenge, Granda
shaving thick curls from a black St. Bruno plug,
packing the wad into his cheek, the pair of them
like squirrels storing sustenance for leaner times.
We would applaud the sizzling of the brown stream
he fired precisely into the roaring fire, run screaming
from his stubbled chin rasping our soft baby cheeks,
shrink from challenges to beat him at hardy knuckles.
And through it all Granny's voice would swaddle us
with love, for Mammy and her six little scallywags.

Denis O'Sullivan

On the Dublin Road

A pint bottle of Strongbow half empty at his feet,
he stands on the leeward side of a phone kiosk,
buttressed against the bonenumbing east wind.
His alcoholic content no protection from the
horizontal sleet, he shivers, eyes frosted with
the winter of his every day,

                    storms of earlier years
hazily recalled, in lines etched deep across his
greyblue cheeks, cyclonic turbulence
in every quiver of his agued limbs:
his future - the half full bottle at his feet.

Denis O'Sullivan

Early Summer

While hawthorn sprayed
the country white as snow,
a café culture blossomed
in the city, adding a soupçon
of the Med to grey pavements.
Glittering discs of aluminium
tables reflected the sun, the
bonhomie of an early summer.
It could have been Paris,
Barcelona, Florence or Milan,
the Spire, our Eiffel Tower,
the Lagan Lady, our David.
How easily we fell for
the cajolery of that single
swooping swallow that had lost
its way!
          June changed all that.
We clutched our cardigans,
wondered if summer would be back
before the year was out.

Denis O'Sullivan

The Visitor

A knock on the door,
at midnight,
shocked me from sleep,
drew me to the window.
My father and the visitor,
mere shadows cast by light
spilling from the hallway,
muttered inaudibly.
The click of the latch
ushered the conversation
inside, defeated my
clandestine eavesdropping.
I tossed beneath the sheets
wallowing in frustration
until I heard the voices raised
and then I knew, I knew.

Denis O'Sullivan

The Belfast Blitz: The Country

Sally Mitchell has a label
pinned to her best green cardigan.
She stands on the platform
ready to be parcelled off
to the country, eyes red,
ringed around with
a knuckled mixture
of tears and grime
and fear.
Sally doesn't even know
where the country is.

Denis O'Sullivan

The Belfast Blitz: Ditchers

John Clark fixes the full moon
through the hawthorn canopy
of the roadside hedge.
His threadbare shirt does little
to keep at bay the April frost.
His wife and two children
shiver beneath his tattered
overcoat, longing for the
warmth of their paupers'
beds, listening for the drone
of the Führer's planes.

Denis O'Sullivan

The Belfast Blitz: First Time

Seán Flynn slings the cardboard box
holding his gasmask
over his skinny shoulder
and carries it proudly to school.
When the master tells the class
to form an orderly line
and not to forget their gasmasks
Seán nearly wets himself with
excitement and anticipation
that at last he will find out
what it's like inside a caravan.

Denis O'Sullivan

The Belfast Blitz: Sleeping Through It

Sleep evades Moyra Woodside
as she lies in bed waiting
for the next bomb, wondering
if her name will be on it,
her resolve draining away
with each shuddering eruption.
At three am, shivering fearfully,
she grabs the whiskey bottle,
swallows a tumblerful neat,
goes to join her husband
sheltering beneath the stairs.

Vital Signs

He left her
disinherited

after he'd plucked her and picked at her
and flung her clothes across the reaped fields,

poisonous gloves
choking her soft summer neck.

Her grubby body lay
where she fell, where I found her –

                    in muddy puddles,
gutted out, run-down, half naked;

her nerve ends raw and reaching out
to the low abandoning sun.

Turn blue planet, turn
and rise like a bubble.

In dark root and space
breathe April, breathe.

Jonathan Hicks

Gone Fishing

Work is just an interruption to you!

Early echoes of youth
surface as I stand on Orlock rocks
hooked to the plunging ocean,

reeling in the steaming tides
under a sky,
battleship grey at times.

*The only thing you'll catch today
is the last bus back to Bangor!*
so I cast further out.

Tramping back, birds are nesting
and the air is Irish seaweed fresh.
Spinner, rod, tackle bag,

the lubricated smell of fresh fish
slipping back in
still hang from my salty mind.

The world has hurled itself away
like spray in the wind
and I do not know or care

if I feel old or young
climbing among these rocks and inlets.
Evening begins to blush.

The coastline is sprinkled in summer rain,
wet barley washes my boots
and all the gorse on sunset fire.

The Bird Trap

Homes hooded in their wimples of snow
overlook the innocent scene and bravado

of young skaters, like the carefree flight
of larks in the warmth of winter sunlight.

The river's frozen surface bears
a weight of gaiety from the villagers

walking on water. But over yonder
the larks, like black leaves have fallen under

the bird trap's invitation: its presence
like the town shrouded in the distance.

Jonathan Hicks

The Maine Man

When the flat-bed lorry drove up our street,
with the soft drink bottles clattering in their crates
we knew: *the Maine man is coming!*

Orangeade, Raspberryade, Brown Lemonade,
sparkling bright as school holidays,
minerals fizzing on our tongues like sherbet dip.

12p a bottle and a penny for empties
we'd set outside the patio door; wind-blown
and clinking around on the tiles for weeks.

We never knew for sure when he'd come:
fortnightly, monthly? the uncertain hour
anticipating the thrill of his return

trading mostly with the Maine man's son
his cool-as-you-like air,
sprawled out over that flat-bed

who didn't like Cream Soda
Wasn't Pop he said
then he'd twist a fresh cap, and I'd hear

the long hiss release Sarsaparilla,
American Cola, Cloudy Limeade; lashing it down
out of the heavens of Ballymoney.

Jonathan Hicks

The Horn

He shuts the door to prayer and privacy,
struts out dressed in his gold and tobacco suit of lights:
a skin as thin as silk, delicately woven in convents
to face the public eye.

Between the pillars of structured society
he firmly stands on his spot, *sol y sombre,* remote
and dangerous centre of attention while commerce,
bikinis and worldly success

around him caress his triumph or tragedy:
Man made perfect in adoration stands before he turns
unbearable and boring. When the horn sinks deep
exposing flesh he'll learn to lose,

his defects inexcusable. The paying horn
and the charging horn will bay for his blood.
He will give them what they came for
and later a good wine will be drunk.

Jonathan Hicks

The Worker

He left
the car keys of his life locked in the car
lost to perpetual notions of escape
with his two pints of anger and a packet of fists, please!
Drunk on doing time, his God-given time!
sold into the slavery of a clock
in, clock out and a grubby wage packet,
gambling the chips of his own freedom,
falling down the man-hole of his own resentment.

> *The wages of sin is death*
> *but the wages in here are worse!*

Boredom laid in like a schoolground bully
coached by staff, trained by school–tie managers,
but he fought back. Took him six years
to knock that job out.

Satie

1
Off-key humour turns
in your one room apartment suites -

creeping with chords
as big as bed bugs - grim

nursery rhymes twinkling in a sky
so distant, so shattered with stars.

2
Sad notes drip from leaves
and off your fingertips
onto the street of your piano.

I stroll with you there
on that grey velvet arm
through the lonely songs of your city.

Jonathan Hicks

My Interior Summer

Dawn puts out the black bin-bags of darkness.

The sun's thumb flips away the moon's counter.
Now my soul peeps out.

Barley fields
are laid out like welcome mats.

Wind grooms the grass
supports the thorn
massages the bark.

Seeds get ready for breeze delivery.

Sap climbs up a tree
just to get away from the world for a while

                    heat drops by all afternoon

roasting the tractor bolts
that plough the flinted heart of my countryside.

Thwarted

I decided to kill her.
She was so lucky, had eyes
fringed with long silky lashes.

My mother, *actually cuddled* her,
said they were beautiful.
'Patsy,' she added, 'has hardly any.'

My heart nearly choked me
with its thuds of black envy.
Stumbling outside,

I searched for a weapon.
My beach things stood waiting,
the pre-war spade, metal and heavy.

I waited, poised by the door.
My mother caught the shaft
before blond curls were bloodied.

Her face had gone all red and twisty,
a terrible screech rushed through her teeth,
her broad hand rose and fell, rose and fell.

The only pain I knew was deep within me.

Pat Taylor

Music Music Music
1937

The music goes round and round
woo - hoo and it comes out here!
Spinning on the wind-up gramophone,
head tilted, a terrier listens to a horn.

***

Beneath the piano, eyes closed,
fingers pressed against the sounding board,
the Lambeth Walk sends rhythm drumming
through my *hap hap happy* bones.

***

Rag time on the wireless! I tap dance
on linoleum. Daddy smiling, lowers his paper,
looks over the top of horn-rimmed glasses,
calls me Shirley Temple.

Pat Taylor

A Game of Joan of Arc 1937

We decided to burn her at the stake.
Joan, the obvious choice,

excited about it herself,
supplied the stinky firelighters.

Just think, if Mrs. Moffett-Chloe
hadn't noticed the smoke

Joan would have been cinders.
We'd have been locked away,

talked about all over the world
in horrified whispers.

Pat Taylor

First Time on a Beach
Eastbourne 1939

A pebbled beach,
sand at the water line
and drowned shoes,
childrens' and grown ups'.
A few still float drifting slowly,
nudged in, drawn back
and finally allowed to rest.

I walk and walk.
This line must stretch
to where the blues all blur.
No one else seems bothered
by sad drowned shoes.
Is every beach like this?

At last I turn.
Crowds of mums and dads.
I've lost myself.
I'm not for crying, that's for sure,
need to find the first
sweet baby boot I'd noticed.
Birds ate Hansel's crumbs
but *I* am following shoes.

The Fairy Boat
1941

I loved my funny, religious Aunt;

blossomed alongside
home-grown Bible stories,

the collection of Doulton ladies,
and china profiles on the wall.

In her bedroom all was pink,
satin-bound blankets, paint,

carpet, even the sharkskin clock.
Each night, kneeling beside

the voluptuous bed, breathing
a mix of Wintergreen liniment

and Evening in Paris,
we'd give our thanks to God.

Wrapped in darkness we'd open
velvet drapes to soft pale light,

climb aboard the fairy boat
and sail towards the August moon:

always I fell asleep too soon.

Scary

My father cleans the grandfather clock.
On the kitchen table its face lies
cushioned on a pile of Derry Standards.
I can read the best now, 'June 5th 1941'.

Mother sits by the green enamelled Tayco-Ette,
a blue Delft bowl fits snugly in her lap,
fingers fly, she's shelling peas,
impatient water spitting from the pot.

I hug our cat; today he wears a frilly bonnet:
his funny, happy song comes buzzing
through my fingers.
I feel so comfortable, so safe, so right.

Oh boy, am I not happy waking old and stiff,
my parents dead, this single bed …

Pat Taylor

Swinging

I don't care what people think,
a lovely stage in life,

as soon as we reach the park
I'm for the nearest swing.

Up, up, up I go, leaning back,
feet heading for the sky,

seventy going on seven,
the inner child is out.

My grandsons are excited,
'Look Mum, *look*! Gran has lift off!'

Christine Leckey

The Rule of St. Benedict

According to Benedict
Christ is in the guest.
Fresh from the shelter,
he came
to celebrate his birthday
at our house.

My Mother's idea.

Presents under the tree.
For him,
a warm coat.
Handy for those
short dark days
on the street.

I got a gold bracelet.

Offerings set before him,
our honoured guest
ate greedily.
Turkey grease dripped
from his yellowed fingers.
No time for conversation.

Fine by me.

Pumpkin pie finished,
he left wearing
the new coat.
Bracelet in the pocket.

Christine Leckey

A Charity Case

On a summer Saturday I cycle
my shiny new Schwinn
up long hills and down short slopes,
a parcel stuffed into my basket,
to Wolcott's Farm. Not much of a place.
Bony cows low in a broken-down barn.
Chickens scratch in the dusty,
cracked yard. An old hound looks dead,
asleep under the rusted pickup.
A heap of kids shout from the house,
that's seen more wind, sun and rain than paint.

From the field, Mr. Wolcott waves,
stripped to the waist, coloured
by the sun and the soil, hard and brown.
You could knock on him, like a door.
Not like my father's soft flesh
stencilled pink, where his golf shirt lets
the summer shine on his office skin.

Mrs. Wolcott gets to the front door
before I do. Baby at her breast,
another in her belly. Steers me
through dirty clothes and kids, apologising
for everything. I hand her the parcel,
she doesn't look inside. Asks if I
have time for a cold drink. Welcome
lemonade in a chipped jelly glass.
'Your mother's a good woman, never
forgot where she came from.' Bet
she wouldn't say that if she could hear
my mother telling her bridge playing
friends about her charity case.

Christine Leckey

Checking Out

He offers me the hire of clean blankets and sheets,
but it's not the time for unnecessary extravagance.
A good deal, the hourly rate at the Paradise Hotel.

I imagine there'll be a tap on the door, a gentle
reminder spoken in a rough voice. Ignored he'll
be back a little later, knock harder, bawl louder.

Likely he'll return for the third time, a charm,
as he tries the door knob and finds it turns easily
in his hand. Shouting 'Hey, mister your time's up.'

If all goes to plan there won't be too much mess.
Quite sure I'm not his first. When he sees the note
he'll mouth 'Oh shit', but know exactly what to do.

Dial 999, the A&E's around the corner, blue light
flash and siren blare. I might even hear it, leaving
the room on my way to explain myself to God.

Christine Leckey

Red Shoes

Today I bought red shoes.
Almost bought a black pair
but plumped for the scarlet because:
black shoes play safe; red shoes have fun.

Red shoes say something about a woman
not said about me in years.
Don't want other men to say it,
my desire is to hear it from you.

Next time we meet I'll wear my red shoes
with a crimson pout to match.
We can start at the top with my lips,
or we can start at the bottom, with my shoes.

I'm easy.
You choose.

Christine Leckey

Small Potatoes

'CLOSED UNTIL FURTHER NOTICE',
pinned to the public house door.
The son of the First & Last is gone.
Wrapped in the metal and glass
he loved to race about the countryside,
dead in a hedge sped past every day.

The first girl my elder son loved
broke his heart. Wounded,
he's determined to break mine.

Small potatoes.
The son of the First & Last is gone,
wrapped in metal and glass.

My younger son: hair long,
conversation short, music loud,
out all hours of the day and night.

Small potatoes.
The son of the First & Last is gone,
wrapped in metal and glass.

Says the bank manager:
'I've rung for a chat'. I know
it'll be more than that.

Small potatoes,
small potatoes.
Smaller.
Tiny potatoes.
Microscopic potatoes.
Truthfully?
No potatoes at all.

Christine Leckey

Sublime in 1999

Wanting a piece of the new market economy,
her husband went from the Midwest to Moscow.
At a loose end, she followed to see what she
might find, away from her friends and the familiar.

Alexei. Employed to drive her husband to and from
the office, the rest of the day he was hers. Some days
he took her shopping, other days he waited outside
five star hotels. She had long liquid lunches with the ladies.

Most days he took her in his tiny apartment
behind the Old Circus. Kneading her tight tennis
playing ass through the never felt melt of silk,
wondering: Do all American women sweat flowers?

He whispered 'Mya kraseeva inistranscia', moaned
as she slid her slender red tipped fingers the length
of his furry thigh, on their way toward his furrier groin.
Funny, this would never have happened in Des Moines.

Christine Leckey

Good in an Emergency

Disassembled,
faith is yanked
from its mooring,
bone is picked
from flesh,
I hear the ambulance
wailing, its wailing:
coming for us.

You died,
or a fine approximation.
I knocked and knocked
on your chest,
willing your heart
to answer.
Head pulled back
to take my mouth;
your life, your death
a breath
apart.

Vivien Paton

Beijing Zoo

Padding from pond to sleeping hut,
hunched in depression,
a lone male Panda;
longing for the bamboo forests of Sichuan
the family, the mountains.

Our Chinese guide smiles,
"British people like animals"
disappointed to see dejected faces.

Vivien Paton

Weather

To-day I am wet and stormy
anger rises, then tears drench my face.
To-morrow I could be sunny,
bask in harmony
or stultify into grey cloudiness.
Contemplative on starry nights,
one with all that is,
I hold on, but it shifts and moves on,
so moving on is all there is.
Move on, move on.

Heimat

Every day I visited
you asked to come home.
The same query, the same hope
my heart breaking on the impossibility,
knowing you would forget
my carefully worded response,
see the light in your eyes when I arrived,
the abandonment as I left.

Grief resolved by years,
I see the abandoned child
was always there.
All your life
reaching towards an illusory place
where pain and panic
would not exist,
where your Mother's arms
would enclose you in sleep
at last, at home.

Love

The sad stalker,
the distraught woman staring at the phone
pose questions about love.

Their lives admit scarcity,
childhood legacy perhaps,
then ironed deeper,
expressed through an emptying out of the heart
to the beloved:

holding nothing back
keeping nothing to sustain
the passage through the tangled forests,
the high mountains of life.

Retreat

Surrounded by lush greenness, shafts of sunlight
alone in my isolated cottage,
I venture a morning pilgrimage to the laughing stream,
sit with feet on a moss covered stone
canopy of filtered blue above.
In my mind the penitent Mary
anoints Christ's feet, and I wonder
if my ragged bundle of sins
will ever be forgiven.
Then, opening chords of the symphony of birds.
Three staccato crochets,
      trill of demi-semi quavers,
          line of repeated quavers,
the melding of many voices:
the making of joyful music.
Aware that sometimes we lose
what we hold dearest,
to uncover the Spirit.

Vivien Paton

Russian Doll

Always a childhood favourite,
an exercise in precision for tiny hands
the excitement of smaller and smaller babushkas
fitting within, to reach the innermost doll,
where nothing divides,
alienation and change
do not threaten,
grief does not destroy,
nor hunger gnaw.

Vivien Paton

The Sky Cage

The canaries of Greece
from narrow cages
in vine covered doorways and tavernas
raise their voices
in jubilant vibrato
through the luminous air.

Circling the planet, their song
past vast galaxies, their music
through the blackness of space, their voices
right to the edge of the universe.

As music is the litany of the spirit
it returns through time
at different pitch and tempo
speaks to every creature
on the road to evolution
lifting a curious head
to hear the canaries song.

Vivien Paton

Wax Wings

It ended in misery, sinking,
unable to keep the impetus,
the fleeting affection
of a self obsessed lover.

Patience and humility only served
to speed the melting of self esteem,
abject failure to grasp the Sun
in a loving embrace,
instead - a crash into
　　　　　　　　the black sea of depression.

Rozana Ahmad Huq

White Shroud

I put on my white shroud,
Wrap it round my body,
Close my eyes
And stop breathing.

There should be lots of flowers
Sweet smell of roses and attar
All around my still body
When you accompany me.

You can hold my hand
It will feel
Lifeless,
And cold to you.

But, I shall feel your warm touch
Seeping through my cold body.

Rozana Ahmad Huq

Just You and Me

When I come home,
I unburden myself
Tell you all the day's events.

I feel tired and I cry
A thousand tears,
But, nobody hears.

Sometimes I think
It's not fair to tell you so much
Of my life's tragedy.

But, when I come home
There's no one there,
Except you.

I talk to you, I tell you things.
I don't know
Why I bother you?

You don't really care.
You sit for awhile,
Selfishly groom yourself.

You have nothing to say.
You just stare
And walk away.

Ready to come back
To fill your belly
When your supper is ready.

Maureen Hill

Wouldya Ouija?

Wouldya dance with me honey
At the Halloween Ball
Wouldya rub bones together
Wouldya come when I call,
Wouldya buy me a ticket
To the necrophiles' rave
Wouldya move the earth for me
Wouldya open my grave
Wouldya tickle my fancy
Wouldya tinkle my bell
Wouldya banish my demons
Wouldya save me from Hell
Wouldya shake, wouldya shimmy
While the saxophones moan
Wouldya cling to me tightly
Tell me I'm not alone
Wouldya press all my buttons
Wouldya stir up my dust
Wouldya scrape off the verdigris
Fire up my lust
Wouldya waltz, wouldya cha cha
Till dawn's early light
Wouldya rock me and roll me
To the end of the night,
And when Halloween's over
And I have to lie down,
Go back to the dark
And my wormeaten gown,
Wouldya pine, wouldya hanker
Refuse to be free
Say yes to my question
Wouldya ouija with me?

Maureen Hill

Memento Mori

On the Falls Road in lunchtime traffic
A Victorian hearse with black plumed horses,
In the limousine behind
Two women gaze out
Like actresses in a play.
My cousin in America insists
Our grandfather had a glass hearse -
I don't think so.
What I remember is the huge dray horses
That came and went outside our house,
Snow sticking to their curved eyelids,
Steam rising from their black nostrils,
And great hooves lifting and falling in slow motion.
In the upstairs bedroom
The children stand awkwardly near the window,
My cousin John is weeping,
I watch the snow drift down,
The strange unearthly light
Falls on the lace inside the coffin.

Now, a lifetime later,
I see my own ten year old face
In the shine of this noonday hearse,
Behind me my uncle stands, tall and dark,
Reflected against the flowers
Of a stranger's funeral .

Maureen Hill

Stage Irish

Sunlight after spring rain.
Puddles of sky light up the road ahead,
Whin bushes flash flakes of fallen sun,
Backlit fields are garish as stained glass,
A dozen honey cows fizz at a gate
A big shouldered tree stands up on points
Ready to pirouette across our path,
We wait for music as we round the bend.

Then someone backstage switches off the lights,
An Irish May slides in monochrome,
The windscreen blurs with coins of drumming rain,
The ragged clack of gusted homing crows
Provides a raucous chorus, a refrain
To open larger spaces in the mind.

We are at home again in the wide skies
And rocky acres of a sombre land,
Unsettled, edgy, washed by stormy seas.
We are vulnerable as seagulls
And as free.

Over the Lough

At the bottom of the hill
Three teenage boys acquire
The accoutrements of dream:
Cheap cans of cider in a brown paper bag,
Climb with their booty
To the castle woods,
To blot out the tedium
Of waiting for their lives to begin.

Next door the zoo teeters over the lough.
In outdoor tenements of meshed light
The lions have resigned themselves to sloth,
Yawn and shiver in October chill,
Growl into fitful sleep,
Dream the gold skies of Africa,
Lope in long strides over the open veldt,
Wake to the smell of northern rains,
The keeper's keys,
A bucket of butcher's slops,
Forgetfulness.

Significant Other

You are always there,
Trapping me in silver shine,
A flat dumb show
Dancing a sinister pavane,
Advance, retreat,
Turn on the pivot of a glance,
A glassy accusing stare,
You wrong foot me at every step.

I put you from me,
Splinter you into spiky fragments
Only to multiply your evil eye,
See myself broken, distorted, gazing back.
Burns had it wrong: we do not want
To see ourselves as others see us,
We want others to see us as we see ourselves,
Or like the Count, that canny fellow,
Not to see ourselves at all.
Instead, I lug you like an extra limb,
The image of a woman I do not know,
A stranger, doppelganger, morbid twin,
Who loiters with intent from dawn to dusk,
Suddenly lunging at me from a window pane,
Or grimacing from the back of a glinting spoon.
When I switch off the light
I know you are waiting, mimicking my breath,
My dark angel, stalker, Sister Self.

Maureen Hill

Buenos Aires

Outside Ricoleta Cemetery
A white boa constrictor
Is casually draped over the shoulder
Of a young man talking to his friends.
I have been to see the tomb of Eva Peron
In a black granite city of mini cathedrals
Under the sun of Capricorn.
Nearby, the statue of tango singer
Carlos Gardel perpetually smokes a lit cigarette-
A more fitting tribute than flowers,
While marble angels soar above.

Everything is nineteen thirties over the top,
I expect to see George Raft and Ray Milland
Among these middle-aged men striking a pose.
Wonderful Latin hair and skin, sharp suits,
A gravitas born of comfort and conformity,
They are performing their Sunday ritual,
Asserting the power of the bourgeoisie,
A social tango perfected over generations.

I applaud their panache, their cool,
They have put their patent heeled stamp
On the silver land,

But out of the corner of my eye
I watch the boa constrictor
And feel a jagged thrill of fear
As it turns on me its alien monster gaze.

Maureen Hill

The World in a Small Room

Dark morning
Water cascades in the radiator,
An ugly gurgling sound.
Reading Robert Lowell's poem
I can feel the cold Atlantic spray
See the oily swell of the whale road
Rippling under the weak stars
As dawn opens the sky above.

The world in a small room.
Lowell, himself passed out of time,
Can pluck me across oceans and centuries
To the Quaker graveyards of Nantucket.
The wind is screeching among the bones of sailors
Mesmerised into eternity by the white whale,
Others lie deep under dark waters,
Become fishes staring ever upwards
At the last lash of the great tail,
Meeting the piteous monster eye
With their own silent cry for mercy,
All are now bone clean,
Scoured to innocence
By the relentless currents
Of tide and time.

In my own pocket of eternity
I wake again
To unheroic wifely tasks
Still carrying in my nostrils
The salty smell of brine.

State of Flow

Successful triple jumpers don't regard
as wasted, months of training, or regret
the sheer hard work and sacrifice required
to master each consecutive component:
the run-up, take-off, rapid hip extension,
'unnatural' landing on the take-off foot,
the bounce, the stretch for ever greater length,
the leg-shoot just before feet hit the sand.

Some can't achieve the synthesis required
to fuse sequential movements into one
symphonic whole, so never do experience
the thrill enjoyed by those who, not constrained
by conscious thought, relax, let go,
and enter an almost mystical state of flow.

Michael Scott

Border Crossing

You always felt a lift, a lightening
on clearing the no-man's land between the posts,
heaved a subconscious sigh of relief
when, sick of the stock reply, the Free State customs
officer waved you through with a bored blind eye.

You knew you'd swapped the 'Six' for 'Twenty-six':
houses in Papal colours, no tricolours,
each post- and 'phone-box over-painted green,
bilingual signs askew, irrelevant,
all roads would take you where you wished to go.

You dodged spring-snapping potholes, middled the road,
(less risk of punctures from dropped horseshoe nails,)
gave way to trustworthy ducks, not fickle chickens,
marvelled at folly of lookalike barking collies
playing Russian roulette with every passing car.

Your Northern sense of urgency ebbed away
when ocean-brightened sky began to loose
your uptight coils: your inner tensions eased
as throat-catch scent of drifting turf smoke fused
with breeze-borne smell of seaweed off Lough Foyle.

You were back where two old men with haltered heifers
could halt your car while they vehemently cursed
the weather and Fine Gael. Not cowed
by your car or moved by your gentle toot, what odds?
Delayed, you were divil-the-bit worse off for that.

The shops and pubs in Carn would still be open,
your welcome, tea and wheaten farls still warm,
the views to Malin just as fine, the sea as
mysterious-- Free State border crossing,
perhaps less on the map than in the mind.

Michael Scott

"Who acts undertakes to suffer". Aeschylus.

Mercy Kick

A wreck of a rabbit cowers by a wall,
sores suppurating, eyes weeping pus:
it suffers in silence, deep in the throes
of myxomatosis.

Keen to despatch the wretched creature
I aim an almighty mercy kick
and connect, but following through smash my toe
on a half-hidden brick.

Michael Scott

A Second Coming

Watching Sputnik streak the evening sky
and time-exposing it, my father
stated he'd like to live to eighty eight.

The satellite has prompted his recall--
a moonless night in Carn: he's twelve,
his father's finger tracking Halley's comet.

He's calculated just how old he'd be
when Halley reappeared, confessed
his hope of living to see a second coming.

Punctually, seventy six years later,
the comet's back; this time my finger
directs his gaze to the barely visible blur;

his age-lined face lights up:
this pale celestial vision
seeming worth a lifetime's wait.

Quizzed about his memories some days on--
first sighting clear,
the longed-for second coming gone.

Mercury

Trembling hands
mirror my mood,
reflect my crumbling
inner mindscape.
Caduceus useless
to chart prognosis,
detect a lifting
of depression,
in desperation
I tap the glass.
Mercury brings
no message of hope:
it's trembling meniscus
mirrors my hands.

Michael Scott

Only a Wren

The freeze-up tightened:
we put out birdseed,
nets of peanuts, fat balls, cheese.
We scattered breadcrumbs,
clearly welcomed,
standing room only on and under
the squirrel-proof table.

Twelve blackbirds
Seven thrushes,
several finches, blue and great tits, two cock robins,
a single wren,
counting discontinued when a magpie
commandeered
the songbirds' station.

Our cat,
the internee, got out:
returned, slunk furtively across the room,
no eye contact.
The ball of feathers in her jaws,
prized loose,
a tattered wren.

Mute, the mite
could barely stand,
shock-shaken, trembling,
tiny bill ajar,
unresponsive,
eyes glazed over,
alive, but only just.

We proffered water,
kept it warm,
withdrew and hoped, to no avail.
We buried it,
strangely affected, though
in the scheme of things,
only a wren.

Brenda Liddy

Butterflies Booming on Bombsites

David Bellamy recalled
a curious fact:
flower seeds
fell from enemy bomb bays
along with the shells, and
London saw another
unintended consequence of war.
Flowers blossomed on the
bombsites, and there was
an excess of
Red Admirals,
Small Tortoiseshells,
Orange Tips,
Painted Ladies,
and Brimstones!

Brenda Liddy

Speculating on Gandhi

He gave away his steel rimmed spectacles for nothing,
and now they are in a New York auction,
along with sandals,
which he walked to freedom in,
and when he didn't need them,
he gave them to a soldier,
he never even sold them.
His pocket watch he kept and always wore
because he never wanted to be late for prayer.

And as for his metal bowl…
I could go on but it would be hyperbole!

I'm sure Gandhi would be amused,
at the fuss over relics that aren't worth two rupees.

Messel Pit

A treasury of fossils,
a cockroach,
a turtle
and a miniature horse
the size of a fox.

Walt Whitman

Before the days of Walkmans,
Wikipedia, ubiquitous
Blackberries, Bebo
Twitter, Flicker and
Facebook,

Walt Whitman
rode around New York in
minibuses, reciting poetry,
and crossing back and forth
on the Brooklyn Ferry,
laughing and singing,
quoting Shakespeare
from scraps of paper
he always carried
in his coat.

After Boston's District Attorney
threatened to ban
Leaves of Grass,
sales were boosted.
Walt pinned a fresh boutonnière
in his lapel and bought
a new house with the proceeds!

Tom Honey

Dandelions

No less a host than Wordsworth's daffodils
you shake your gold umbrellas in the sun.
Yes, dandelions, propagate yourselves,
the sight of yellow multitudes can stun.
You know, in spite of humble origins,
that you are fit to colonise the earth.
It's true, sometimes, the garden sprayer wins.
But what's a small defeat? You know your worth.

You bloom in spite of rubble at your feet.
You burst through concrete crevices, ignore
the strewn carry-outs, the dirty street
and smile, for you have seen it all before.
You send your wingéd children through the air
and bless them with a dandelion prayer.

Surreal

In the Dali Museum, Figueres

The nude, back view only shown,
looks through the canvas
as if held by something beyond.
She stands hemmed by paint spilt
in many coloured patches
like a luminous quilt.
Cameras are raised all around her
but no one clicks or flashes.
Look through your view finder.
We do, and gasp, blinking
at what we see. No nude,
but the face of Abraham Lincoln!
Dali, somewhere in the other world,
gives his asymmetric 'tache a twirl

Starlings

Scout on the roof chirps "Grub!"
and from hidden sky-holes the starlings fall
to swagger to their local pub.

My garden plot! There they have a ball,
gobbling morsels meant for the timid sort.
A real vacuum job, then they're off in a squall.

No opportunity lost, they soon resort
to similar raids on another's patch,
a pirate plan for every port.

When they sing the blackbird is no match
for their unmelodious chorus, full vibrato.
They sizzle! A performance to watch.

Committed to their own libretto,
boy, do they have a fling,
raising the roof in their mobile ghetto.

Between them and me, it's a love-hate thing.

Tom Honey

The Lazy Versemaker's Villanelle

Carpe Diem sounds an urgent note
and his intentions are to seize the day.
Too often, though, he's sure to miss the boat.

He starts, of course, by taking off his coat
as if he's out to trigger an affray.
Carpe Diem sounds an urgent note.

He talks about the poems he nearly wrote,
convinced that most of them would be okay.
Too often, though, he's sure to miss the boat.

Imagination sets his thoughts afloat.
Increasingly they seem to go astray.
Carpe Diem sounds an urgent note.

He trawls through Shakespeare for a useful quote,
a phrase to prod his own muse into play.
Too often, though, he's sure to miss the boat

It seems of late he simply works by rote,
more and more conscious of his feet of clay.
Carpe Diem sounds an urgent note.
Too often, though, he's sure to miss the boat.

All the Hands

"Nobody likes me, sir", he said
standing at my desk. I suspected
it was true, but denied it.
"Nonsense, Seánie, don't I like you?"

Next day, school outing. He'd come
empty-handed, his shirt flying,
not a button left on it.
No togs, no gear, no lunch.

"Seánie has no lunch. Who can help?"
Up shot the hands. More than half the class.
Mars bars, Kit Kats, Chews, Coke,
landed on his desk.

A wholly happy day by the sea. Afterwards,
"Well, Seánie, what do you remember most?"
"All the hands sir," he said
Yes, Seánie, all the hands.

Tom Honey

Latitudes 1

Three mounted gauchos pass, sombreroed,
tented in thick ponchos that droop
to stirrup level. They ride, bowed
into the wind that rakes the pampas
and against which my long overcoat
makes no defence. Thin shoes drink
mud that hooves have churned.

No comfort promised in homes ahead
for all are hearthless, and suddenly
I'm stabbed with longings for nights
back in Belfast round the fire,
butter melting on a plate of toast,
a mug of cocoa in my hand.

Tom Honey

Latitudes 2

Worth the short trip from Macapá,
we thought, to stand beside the posts
marking the line and feel equator heat.
It was a stretch of scrubby ground
without trees, so we were exposed,
but the high sun that day
did not lean heavily on us.
Our shadows curled like cats about
our feet. A light wind, coming from
the coast where Amazon took on
the Atlantic, tempered the air.
We felt at ease, took photos
of each other, drove off content
that we had not been bested by the heat
while sampling zero latitude.

Robert Kirk

A Mourne Myth

We lay down
like Gods on the summit
of Meelbeg, with Bearnagh behind us
adorned with craggy crown;
and surveyed the world below,
as we plotted intricate seams
of gold to guide us homeward
between the jigsaw of fields.

We came down
a granite strewn ridge
and entered the silent labyrinth
walled with hawthorn and whin.
But soon the peace was broken,
by echoes of dreadful bellowing.

We came across
the place of pain;
found Theseus, triumphant,
armed with jagged saw in bloodied hand;
and caged in steel, the Minotaur, wounded
head locked between the bars, denuded;
as circlets of horn welled blood and flowed
over fearful eyes and blotted the barren ground
where lay the hollow crown.

Robert Kirk

Alternative Reality

Reclusive:
bedroom exclusive,
her inner space
within the fabric
of the universe.
She is sun:
nuclear reactions.
She is moon:
cold and wan.
She is goddess
to alternative reality
enlivened by microchip
technology; as circuitry
makes and breaks
directing jerky automatons
across a monitor stage.
Caveat: virtual families
demand observation
or they'll perish.
No matter!
Shut down!
Re-boot!
Begin again!

Cerebral Death

Below a turnip lantern moon,
spiders spin fragile webs, painted
hoary by night's cold breath, dressed
the hawthorn in gossamer threads,
beaded red; pointed with thorns.

Morning sun, disrobed of pallid shroud
dissolved ethereal strands, but set ablaze
a crimson acer; burned a funeral pyre.

Witnessed the end:

Lines linked to life
severed from limbs still warm
and yellowed like old newspapers
under a carpet; last gasp a whisper
of crisp leaves crushed underfoot;
behind dead blue eyes, every thought
ever had, begins to moulder.

Did not die in the public eye!
Was not famous for fifteen minutes!
Did not have flowers flung onto a hearse!
Was not celebrated by the tabloid press!

Died unnoticed.

No pronouncements:
Only the thrum of pipes
expanding under bedroom boards
and a raucous choir in the garden:
grey crows perched in the beeches.

Gave verse to a phoney world.
Died unvoiced.

Leaving Finvoy Street

Time of departure,
daylight darkens heavy
black clouds slump
above rooftops to dump
more rain upon the street
and ripple the puddles.

Row on row,
tedious blue-black slates
glisten like an oil spill
on the Lagan; and wind
moans among branches
of aerials stained with soot,
and wails a lament over cold lips
of terracotta chimney pots.

Side by side – blind and mute,
terraced memories vacated;
tried and condemned by avarice,
they await demolition.

He did not look
back and see a red door
reflect on damp tarmac.

Vivien Paton lives in South Belfast. She has written three books for children and is working on a picture alphabet for her granddaughter. In poetry, Vivien is interested in exploring human relationships, especially pivotal moments that change the pattern or direction of a life. She finds inspiration also in growing things, animals and the spiritual life.

Brenda Liddy has published two books *Women's Sevententh Century Drama.* New York: Cambria Press, 2008. *The Drama of War in the Theatre of Anne Devlin, Marie Jones, and Christina Reid, Three Irish Playwrights.* Lampeter: Mellon Press, 2009.

Maureen Hill was born and grew up in Belfast. She has published articles and poems in various magazines including South and The Seventh Quarry.

Michael Scott was born in Derry and went to school in Armagh. His poems have been published in Ulla's Nib, the Irish Medical Journal, the Belfast Newsletter and Blythe Spirit.

Noreen Campbell has been published in BIFHE anthologies (1998 and 1999) and *Turning Point*(2007), in New Belfast Community Arts Initiative Poetry in Motion projects: *Glass Sculpture* (2001), *Lonely Poets Guide to Belfast* (2003), *BT1* (2005), in Shalom House Poetry anthologies: *Keeping the Colours New* (2003), *A Trail of Silver Papers* (2007), in *My Story* BBC publications 2006.
She also published a book of poetry and short stories *The Shore Fields* jointly with Denis O'Sullivan (2006)

Pat Taylor's poems have been published in Gown, Honest Ulsterman, CWN Magazine and various anthologies.
Her poem *And so On* was chosen to be engraved in a glass sculpture as part of New Belfast Community Arts Initiative (2001), and her poem *Bereft* helped to inspire the design for a memorial window in Belfast City Hall, by artist Nora Gaston.
Shalom House Poetry published Pat's first collection *Just as it Was* in 2005. A second collection is nearing completion.

Rozana Ahmad Huq writes poetry and short stories. Her work has been published in magazines, journals, anthologies and featured in

BBC broadcasts. Rozana has performed poetry, stories, music and dance in a number of community arts and festival events.
Born in Bangladesh but living in Northern Ireland, she takes her inspiration from both cultures.

Denis O'Sullivan has published a book of short stories and poetry *The Shore Fields* jointly with Noreen Campbell and has featured in Shalom House Poetry's anthologies *Keeping the Colours New* and *A Trail of Silver Papers*. He has also been published in several Community Arts Initiative projects, in the BBC publication *My Story, Ireland's Own* and *The Black Mountain Review*

Jonathan Hicks lives in Belfast so far... works hard at doing nothing, and often wonders how his poems get published at all! Despite that, he's won a few local competitions and his booklet *Love in the Time of Doubt* was published in 2006. He writes songs and plays in his band *Jonee's Mum*.

Robert Cecil Kirk is married to Isabel and lives in Ballygowan. He started writing poetry in 2008 but has only recently had the confidence to let others view his work. Pastimes include mountain walking, gardening, reading and, most obviously, writing.

Christine Leckey was born and grew up in Massachusetts. Except for a few years spent in Russia and Romania, Northern Ireland has been her home all of her adult life. She is married with two grown-up sons.